YOU KNOW WHEN YOU'RE IN LOVE WHEN

Reality is finally better than your dreams

Dr. Seuss

THIS BUCKET LIST IS THE CREATION OF

AND

IF FOUND, PLEASE CONTACT US URGENTLY:

THE MASTER LIST

PAGE	ACTIVITY	DONE
2		
3		
4		
5		
6		
7		
8		
9		
10		
11		
12		
13		
14		
15		
16		
17		
18		
19		
20		
21		
22		
23		
24		
25		
26		

PAGE	ACTIVITY	DONE
27		
28		
29		
30		
31		
32		
33		
34		
35		
36		
37		
38		
39		
40		
41		
42		
43		
44		
45		
46		
47		
48		
49		
50		
51		

THE MASTER LIST

PAGE	ACTIVITY	DONE
52		
53		
54		
55		
56		
57		
58		
59		
60		
61		
62		
63		
64		
65		
66		
67		
68		
69		
70		
71		
72		
73		
74		
75		
76		

PAGE	ACTIVITY	DONE
77		
78		
79		
80		
81		
82		
83		
84		
85		
86		
87		
88		
89		
90		
91		
92		
93		
94		
95		
96		
97		
98		
99		
100		
101		

IDEA TRIGGERS

ACCOLADE	CREATE	FASCINATING	HOP	MASS	PRECIOUS	REUNIFY	START BALL
ACCOMPLISH	CROWD	FASHION	HOT	MATCH	PREPARED	REUNITE	ROLLING
ACCUMULATE	CRUISING	FATHER	HUDDLE	MATTER	PROBE	REVAMP	START OFF
ACQUIRE	CULTIVATE	FEARLESS	HUMOR	MEET	PROCLAIM	REVEL	STATION
ACT	CURIOUS	FEAST	HUNT	MEET AGAIN	PROCREATE	REVERE	STAY
ACTUALIZE	CUTE	FEAT	IMAGINE	MEMORIALIZE	PRODUCE	REVISE	STEAMY
AD-LIB	DALLIANCE	FEATHER IN CAP	IMPRESS	MEND	PROGRESS	REVITALIZE	STIMULATE
ADVANCE	DAUNTLESS	FESTIVITY	IMPROVE	MERRIMENT	PROJECT	REVIVE	STIR
ADVENTURE	DECISION	FETCHING	IMPROVISE	MERRYMAKING	PROMOTE	RIDE	STOCKPILE
AFFECT CHANGE	DECORATION	FIND	INCIDENT	MILESTONE	PROMPT	RIDING	STOPOVER
AGGREGATE	DEDICATE	FINISH	INCLINED	MIRACLE	PROPEL	RING IN	STORY
ALLURING	DEED	FIRE UP	INCREASE	MOBILIZE	PROSPECT	RISK	STRAIGHTEN OUT
AMASS	DELECTABLE	FIX	INDIVIDUAL	MOOR	PROVIDE	RISQUÉ	STRANGE
AMBROSIAL	DELICIOAUS	FLING	INFLUENCE	MOTIVATE	PROVOCATIVE	ROMANTIC	STRIKE
AMEND	DELIGHT	FLIRTATIOUS	INFORM	MOVE	PROVOKING	ROMP	STRIKING
AMUSEMENT	DELIGHTFUL	FLOCK	INFUSE	MOVEMENT	PUBLICIZE	ROUND UP	SUAVE
ANNIVERSARY	DELIVER	FLYING	INITIATE	MUSTER	PUNCH	ROUSE	SUGGESTIVE
APPEALING	DELVE INTO	FOLLOW	INQUIRING	NAVIGATION	PURIFY	SABBATICAL	SWARM
APPEARANCE	DESIGN	THROUGH	INQUISITIVE	NEGOTIATE	PURSUIT	SAILING	SWING
AROUSE	DESIROUS	FOOLERY	INSPECT	NERVY	PUT	SCARE	TAKE OFF
ASSOCIATE	DEVELOP	FOREIGN	INSPIRIT	OBSERVE	PUZZLED	SCENE	TEASING
ATHLETICS	DEVISE	FORGE	INSTALL	OBTAIN	QUESTIONING	SCHEME	TEST
ATTAIN	DIFFERENT	FORM	INSTILL	OCCASION	QUICKEN	SCHOLARSHIP	THING
AVANT GARDE	DIG INTO	FORMULATE	INSTITUTE	OCCUPATION	QUIET	SCOPE	THRONG
BETTER	DISCOVER	FRAME	INTERESTED	OCCURRENCE	RACK UP	SCORE	THROW DICE
BIKING	DISCOVERY	FREEDOM	INTREPID	OFF-THE-CUFF	RACY	SCOUT	TIME OFF
BIZARRE	DISHY	FRISK	INTRODUCED	ONE AND ONLY	RAFFLE	SEAFARING	TITILLATING
BLESS	DISPORT	FROLIC	INVENT	OPPORTUNITY	RAISE	SEAL	TOUCH
BOLD	DISPOSED	FULFILL	INVEST	ORDER	RAISE HELL	SEARCH	TOUCH UP
BOOST	DISTINCTION	FUN	INVIGORATE	ORGANIZE	RALLY	SECURE	TOUR
BREAKTHROUGH	DISTRACTION	GAIN	INVITE	ORIGINATE	RAMBLE	SEDUCTIVE	TRANSIT
BRING ABOUT	DIVERSION	GAIN GROUND	JEST	OUTLANDISH	RARE	SEEK	TRAVEL
BUILD	DO	GALLANT	JOIN	OUTSIDE CHANCE	REACH	SENSUAL	TRAVERSE
BURROW	DONATION	GALVANIZE	JOKE	OVERHAUL	REACTIVATE	SET DOWN	TREKKING
BUSINESS	DREAM UP	GAME	JOKING	OVERNIGHT	READY	SET IN MOTION	TRIP
CALL UP	DREAMY	GAMING	JUBILATE	PAINT TOWN RED	REALIZE	SET RIGHT	TRIUMPH
CAPER	DRINK TO	GENERATE	JUNKET	PARENT	REASSEMBLE	SET UP	TROPHY
CAPTIVATING	DRIVE	GET	KEEP	PARTY	REASSURE	SETTLE	TRY
CAPTURE	EAGER	GET DONE	KICK UP HEELS	PASS	RECESS	SEXY	TURN ON
CAROUSE	EARN WINGS	GET TOGETHER	KINKY	PASSAGE	RECONCILE	SHAPE UP	TURNING POINT
CAUSE	EFFECT	GIFT	KISSABLE	PASTIME	RECONDITION	SHARPEN	UNAFRAID
CELEBRATION	ELATE	GIVE LIFE TO	LAND	PATCH UP	RECONVENE	SHIFT	UNCOMMON
CEREMONY	ELEVATE	GIVE RISE TO	LANDMARK	PAUSE	RECOVER	SHOT IN THE DARK	UNDERTAKING
CHANCE	EMBOLDEN	GLAMOROUS	LARK	PECULIAR	RECREATE	SIGHTSEEING	UNFAMILIAR
CHARMING	ENACT	GLOBE-TROTTING	LAUD	PEREGRINE	RECREATION	SIGN	UNFLINCHING
CHOOSE	ENDOWMENT	GLORIFY	LAY FOUNDATION	PERFECT	RECTIFY	SIRE	UNITE
CIRCUMSTANCE	ENERGIZE	GO INTO	LEAP	PERFORM	RECUPERATE	SITUATION	UNUSUAL
CLEANSE	ENHANCE	GOLD STAR	LET LOOSE	PERK UP	REFINE	SKYROCKET	UP FOR
CLUSTER	ENKINDLE	GRANT	LIBIDINOUS	PERSEVERING	REFORM	SOJOURN	UPGRADE
COINCIDENCE	ENLIVEN	GROUND	LINE	PERSISTENT	REFRESH	SOLVE	VACATION
COLLECT	ENTERPRISE	GROUP	LIVE	PHASE	REFURBISH	SPARE MOMENTS	VALIANT
COLORFUL	ENTICING	HALLOW	LIVE IT UP	PHENOMENON	REJOICE	SPARE TIME	VALOROUS
COME UP WITH	ENVISION	HANG AROUND	LODGE	PICK UP	REJOIN	SPARK	VENTURE
COME-HITHER	ESTABLISH	HANG OUT	LONG SHOT	PILE UP	REKINDLE	SPAWN	VOYAGE
COMPLETE	EVENING	HAPPENING	LOOK INTO	PLACE	RELAXATION	SPEC	WAGER
COMPOSE	EVENT	HAPPINESS	LOOK UP	PLAN	REMAKE	SPECULATION	WALK
CONCEIVE	EXALT	HARDY	LOTTERY	PLAY	REMODEL	SPICY	WANDER
CONCENTRATE	EXAMINE	HATCH	LUSCIOUS	PLEASING	RENEW	SPIRITED	WANDERLUST
CONCLUDE	EXCITE	HAVE A BALL	MAKE	PLEASURE	REPAIR	SPORT	WAY OUT
CONCOCT	EXCLUSIVE	HAVE A LOOK	MAKE MERRY	PLUCK	RESEARCH	SPORTS	WAYFARING
CONGREGATE	EXCURSION	HEAP	MAKE OVER	PLUCKY	RESOLUTE	SPRUCE	WEEKEND
CONSECRATE	EXHILARATE	HEARTEN	MAKE STRIDES	POKE	RESOLVE	SPRUCE UP	WEIRD
CONSTRUCT	EXPEDITION	HEAVENLY	MAKE THE SCENE	POLISH	REST	SPUNKY	WIN
CONTINGENCY	EXPERIENCE	HELP	MAKE UP	POUR IN	RESTORE	SPUR	WING
CONVERGE	EXTERNAL	HEROIC	MAKE WHOOPEE	PRACTICE	RESURRECT	STABILIZE	WONDER
COOK UP	EXTRAORDINARY	HOLIDAY	MANAGE	PRAISE	RETIREMENT	STACK UP	WORK UP
COURAGEOUS	FAR OUT	HONOR	MARVEL	PRANK	RETRIEVE	START	WRITE

THIS WOULD BE PERFECT FOR US BECAUSE...

_____

_____

_____

_____

MAKE IT HAPPEN: HOW? WHEN?

_____

_____

_____

_____

REVIEW

DATE COMPLETED: / /

_____

WHAT HAPPENED? (PEOPLE MET, HIGH POINTS, CHALLENGES, EXPECTATIONS VS REALITY)

_____

_____

_____

_____

THE **BEST PART** WAS...

_____

_____

_____

_____

_____

BUDGET

$

ANTICIPATED DATE

/ /   TO   / /

ACTION LIST

⊘
⊘
⊘
⊘
⊘
⊘
⊘
⊘
⊘

SUCCESS!

PLACE A CHECK HERE TO
TAKE IT OFF YOUR BUCKET LIST

RATE THIS ACTIVITY

☆☆☆☆☆

THIS WOULD BE PERFECT FOR US BECAUSE...

_____
_____
_____
_____

MAKE IT HAPPEN: HOW? WHEN?

_____
_____
_____
_____
_____

REVIEW

DATE COMPLETED: / /

WHAT HAPPENED? (PEOPLE MET, HIGH POINTS, CHALLENGES, EXPECTATIONS VS REALITY)

_____
_____
_____
_____

THE **BEST PART** WAS...

_____
_____
_____
_____

BUDGET

$

ANTICIPATED DATE

/ /   TO   / /

ACTION LIST

⊘
⊘
⊘
⊘
⊘
⊘
⊘
⊘
⊘

SUCCESS!

PLACE A CHECK HERE TO
TAKE IT OFF YOUR BUCKET LIST

RATE THIS ACTIVITY

☆☆☆☆☆

THIS WOULD BE PERFECT FOR US BECAUSE...

_____

_____

_____

MAKE IT HAPPEN: HOW? WHEN?

_____

_____

_____

_____

REVIEW

DATE COMPLETED: / /

_____

WHAT HAPPENED? (PEOPLE MET, HIGH POINTS, CHALLENGES, EXPECTATIONS VS REALITY)

_____

_____

_____

_____

THE **BEST PART** WAS...

_____

_____

_____

_____

_____

BUDGET

$

ANTICIPATED DATE

/ /   TO   / /

ACTION LIST

⊘
⊘
⊘
⊘
⊘
⊘
⊘
⊘
⊘

SUCCESS!

PLACE A CHECK HERE TO
TAKE IT OFF YOUR BUCKET LIST

RATE THIS ACTIVITY

☆☆☆☆☆

THIS WOULD BE PERFECT FOR US BECAUSE...

_____

_____

_____

_____

MAKE IT HAPPEN: HOW? WHEN?

_____

_____

_____

_____

REVIEW

DATE COMPLETED: / /

_____

WHAT HAPPENED? (PEOPLE MET, HIGH POINTS, CHALLENGES, EXPECTATIONS VS REALITY)

_____

_____

_____

_____

THE **BEST PART** WAS...

_____

_____

_____

_____

_____

BUDGET

$

ANTICIPATED DATE

/ /   TO   / /

ACTION LIST

⊘
⊘
⊘
⊘
⊘
⊘
⊘
⊘
⊘

SUCCESS!

PLACE A CHECK HERE TO
TAKE IT OFF YOUR BUCKET LIST

RATE THIS ACTIVITY

☆☆☆☆☆

PRIORITY ☆☆☆☆☆   ITEM #5: _____

THIS WOULD BE PERFECT FOR US BECAUSE...

_____
_____
_____
_____

MAKE IT HAPPEN: HOW? WHEN?

_____
_____
_____
_____

REVIEW

DATE COMPLETED: / /

WHAT HAPPENED? (PEOPLE MET, HIGH POINTS, CHALLENGES, EXPECTATIONS VS REALITY)

_____
_____
_____
_____

THE **BEST PART** WAS...

_____
_____
_____
_____
_____

BUDGET
$

ANTICIPATED DATE

/ /   TO   / /

ACTION LIST

- ⊘
- ⊘
- ⊘
- ⊘
- ⊘
- ⊘
- ⊘
- ⊘
- ⊘

SUCCESS!

PLACE A CHECK HERE TO
TAKE IT OFF YOUR BUCKET LIST

RATE THIS ACTIVITY

☆☆☆☆☆

ITEM #6: _____

THIS WOULD BE PERFECT FOR US BECAUSE...

_____
_____
_____
_____

MAKE IT HAPPEN: HOW? WHEN?

_____
_____
_____
_____
_____

REVIEW

DATE COMPLETED: / /

_____

WHAT HAPPENED? (PEOPLE MET, HIGH POINTS, CHALLENGES, EXPECTATIONS VS REALITY)

_____
_____
_____
_____
_____

THE **BEST PART** WAS...

_____
_____
_____
_____
_____

BUDGET

$

ANTICIPATED DATE

/ /   TO   / /

ACTION LIST

⊘
⊘
⊘
⊘
⊘
⊘
⊘
⊘
⊘

SUCCESS!

PLACE A CHECK HERE TO
TAKE IT OFF YOUR BUCKET LIST

RATE THIS ACTIVITY

☆☆☆☆☆

THIS WOULD BE PERFECT FOR US BECAUSE...

_____
_____
_____

MAKE IT HAPPEN: HOW? WHEN?

_____
_____
_____
_____

REVIEW

DATE COMPLETED: / /

WHAT HAPPENED? (PEOPLE MET, HIGH POINTS, CHALLENGES, EXPECTATIONS VS REALITY)

_____
_____
_____
_____

THE **BEST PART** WAS...

_____
_____
_____
_____

BUDGET

$

ANTICIPATED DATE

/ /   TO   / /

ACTION LIST

⊘
⊘
⊘
⊘
⊘
⊘
⊘
⊘
⊘

SUCCESS!

PLACE A CHECK HERE TO
TAKE IT OFF YOUR BUCKET LIST

RATE THIS ACTIVITY

☆☆☆☆☆

I'VE MISSED MORE THAN 9000 SHOTS IN MY CAREER. I'VE LOST ALMOST 300 GAMES. 26 TIMES I'VE BEEN TRUSTED TO TAKE THE GAME WINNING SHOT AND MISSED. I'VE FAILED OVER AND OVER AND OVER AGAIN IN MY LIFE. AND THAT IS WHY I SUCCEED. — MICHAEL JORDAN

7

THIS WOULD BE PERFECT FOR US BECAUSE...

_____

_____

_____

MAKE IT HAPPEN: HOW? WHEN?

_____

_____

_____

_____

REVIEW

DATE COMPLETED: / /

WHAT HAPPENED? (PEOPLE MET, HIGH POINTS, CHALLENGES, EXPECTATIONS VS REALITY)

_____

_____

_____

_____

THE **BEST PART** WAS...

_____

_____

_____

_____

BUDGET

$

ANTICIPATED DATE

/ /   TO   / /

ACTION LIST

⊘
⊘
⊘
⊘
⊘
⊘
⊘
⊘
⊘

SUCCESS!

PLACE A CHECK HERE TO
TAKE IT OFF YOUR BUCKET LIST

RATE THIS ACTIVITY

☆☆☆☆☆

PRIORITY ☆☆☆☆☆   ITEM #9: _____

THIS WOULD BE PERFECT FOR US BECAUSE...	**BUDGET**

BUDGET

$

ANTICIPATED DATE

/ /   TO   / /

MAKE IT HAPPEN: HOW? WHEN?

ACTION LIST

⊘
⊘
⊘
⊘
⊘
⊘
⊘
⊘
⊘

REVIEW

DATE COMPLETED: / /

WHAT HAPPENED? (PEOPLE MET, HIGH POINTS, CHALLENGES, EXPECTATIONS VS REALITY)

SUCCESS!

PLACE A CHECK HERE TO
TAKE IT OFF YOUR BUCKET LIST

THE **BEST PART** WAS...

RATE THIS ACTIVITY

☆☆☆☆☆

THIS WOULD BE PERFECT FOR US BECAUSE...

| | **BUDGET** |
| | $ |

ANTICIPATED DATE

/ /   TO   / /

MAKE IT HAPPEN: HOW? WHEN?

ACTION LIST

⊘
⊘
⊘
⊘
⊘
⊘
⊘
⊘
⊘

REVIEW

DATE COMPLETED: / /

WHAT HAPPENED? (PEOPLE MET, HIGH POINTS, CHALLENGES, EXPECTATIONS VS REALITY)

SUCCESS!

PLACE A CHECK HERE TO
TAKE IT OFF YOUR BUCKET LIST

THE **BEST PART** WAS...

RATE THIS ACTIVITY

☆☆☆☆☆

THIS WOULD BE PERFECT FOR US BECAUSE...

_____

_____

_____

_____

MAKE IT HAPPEN: HOW? WHEN?

_____

_____

_____

_____

REVIEW

DATE COMPLETED: /   /

_____

WHAT HAPPENED? (PEOPLE MET, HIGH POINTS, CHALLENGES, EXPECTATIONS VS REALITY)

_____

_____

_____

_____

THE **BEST PART** WAS...

_____

_____

_____

_____

_____

BUDGET

$

ANTICIPATED DATE

/ /   TO   / /

ACTION LIST

⊘
⊘
⊘
⊘
⊘
⊘
⊘
⊘
⊘

SUCCESS!

PLACE A CHECK HERE TO
TAKE IT OFF YOUR BUCKET LIST

RATE THIS ACTIVITY

☆☆☆☆☆

THIS WOULD BE PERFECT FOR US BECAUSE...

MAKE IT HAPPEN: HOW? WHEN?

REVIEW

DATE COMPLETED: / /

WHAT HAPPENED? (PEOPLE MET, HIGH POINTS, CHALLENGES, EXPECTATIONS VS REALITY)

THE **BEST PART** WAS...

BUDGET

$

ANTICIPATED DATE

/ /   TO   / /

ACTION LIST

- ⊘
- ⊘
- ⊘
- ⊘
- ⊘
- ⊘
- ⊘
- ⊘
- ⊘

SUCCESS!

PLACE A CHECK HERE TO
TAKE IT OFF YOUR BUCKET LIST

RATE THIS ACTIVITY

☆☆☆☆☆

PRIORITY ☆☆☆☆☆   ITEM #13: _____

THIS WOULD BE PERFECT FOR US BECAUSE...	**BUDGET**
	$
	ANTICIPATED DATE
	/ / TO / /
MAKE IT HAPPEN: HOW? WHEN?	**ACTION LIST**

⊘
⊘
⊘
⊘
⊘
⊘
⊘
⊘
⊘

REVIEW

DATE COMPLETED: / /

WHAT HAPPENED? (PEOPLE MET, HIGH POINTS, CHALLENGES, EXPECTATIONS VS REALITY)

SUCCESS!

PLACE A CHECK HERE TO
TAKE IT OFF YOUR BUCKET LIST

THE **BEST PART** WAS...

RATE THIS ACTIVITY

☆☆☆☆☆

THIS WOULD BE PERFECT FOR US BECAUSE...

_____
_____
_____
_____

MAKE IT HAPPEN: HOW? WHEN?

_____
_____
_____
_____
_____

REVIEW

DATE COMPLETED: / /

_____

WHAT HAPPENED? (PEOPLE MET, HIGH POINTS, CHALLENGES, EXPECTATIONS VS REALITY)

_____
_____
_____
_____
_____

THE **BEST PART** WAS...

_____
_____
_____
_____
_____

BUDGET

$

ANTICIPATED DATE

/ /   TO   / /

ACTION LIST

⊘
⊘
⊘
⊘
⊘
⊘
⊘
⊘
⊘

SUCCESS!

PLACE A CHECK HERE TO
TAKE IT OFF YOUR BUCKET LIST

RATE THIS ACTIVITY

☆☆☆☆☆

TWENTY YEARS FROM NOW YOU WILL BE MORE DISAPPOINTED BY THE THINGS THAT YOU DIDN'T DO
THAN BY THE ONES YOU DID DO, SO THROW OFF THE BOWLINES, SAIL AWAY FROM SAFE HARBOR,
CATCH THE TRADE WINDS IN YOUR SAILS: EXPLORE, DREAM, DISCOVER. – MARK TWAIN

PRIORITY ☆☆☆☆☆   ITEM #15: _____

THIS WOULD BE PERFECT FOR US BECAUSE...

_____
_____
_____

MAKE IT HAPPEN: HOW? WHEN?

_____
_____
_____
_____

REVIEW

DATE COMPLETED: /   /

WHAT HAPPENED? (PEOPLE MET, HIGH POINTS, CHALLENGES, EXPECTATIONS VS REALITY)

_____
_____
_____
_____

THE **BEST PART** WAS...

_____
_____
_____
_____
_____

BUDGET

$

ANTICIPATED DATE

/ /   TO   / /

ACTION LIST

⊘
⊘
⊘
⊘
⊘
⊘
⊘
⊘
⊘

SUCCESS!

PLACE A CHECK HERE TO
TAKE IT OFF YOUR BUCKET LIST

RATE THIS ACTIVITY

☆☆☆☆☆

THIS WOULD BE PERFECT FOR US BECAUSE...

_____

_____

_____

MAKE IT HAPPEN: HOW? WHEN?

_____

_____

_____

_____

REVIEW

DATE COMPLETED: /   /

WHAT HAPPENED? (PEOPLE MET, HIGH POINTS, CHALLENGES, EXPECTATIONS VS REALITY)

_____

_____

_____

_____

_____

THE **BEST PART** WAS...

_____

_____

_____

_____

_____

BUDGET

$

ANTICIPATED DATE

/   /   TO   /   /

ACTION LIST

⊘
⊘
⊘
⊘
⊘
⊘
⊘
⊘
⊘

SUCCESS!

PLACE A CHECK HERE TO
TAKE IT OFF YOUR BUCKET LIST

RATE THIS ACTIVITY

☆☆☆☆☆

THIS WOULD BE PERFECT FOR US BECAUSE...

MAKE IT HAPPEN: HOW? WHEN?

REVIEW

DATE COMPLETED: / /

WHAT HAPPENED? (PEOPLE MET, HIGH POINTS, CHALLENGES, EXPECTATIONS VS REALITY)

THE **BEST PART** WAS...

BUDGET

$

ANTICIPATED DATE

/ /   TO   / /

ACTION LIST

⊘
⊘
⊘
⊘
⊘
⊘
⊘
⊘
⊘

SUCCESS!

PLACE A CHECK HERE TO
TAKE IT OFF YOUR BUCKET LIST

RATE THIS ACTIVITY

☆☆☆☆☆

THIS WOULD BE PERFECT FOR US BECAUSE...

_____

_____

_____

_____

MAKE IT HAPPEN: HOW? WHEN?

_____

_____

_____

_____

_____

REVIEW

DATE COMPLETED: / /

_____

WHAT HAPPENED? (PEOPLE MET, HIGH POINTS, CHALLENGES, EXPECTATIONS VS REALITY)

_____

_____

_____

_____

_____

THE **BEST PART** WAS...

_____

_____

_____

_____

_____

_____

BUDGET

$

ANTICIPATED DATE

/ /   TO   / /

ACTION LIST

⊘
⊘
⊘
⊘
⊘
⊘
⊘
⊘
⊘

SUCCESS!

PLACE A CHECK HERE TO
TAKE IT OFF YOUR BUCKET LIST

RATE THIS ACTIVITY

☆☆☆☆☆

THIS WOULD BE PERFECT FOR US BECAUSE...

MAKE IT HAPPEN: HOW? WHEN?

REVIEW

DATE COMPLETED: / /

WHAT HAPPENED? (PEOPLE MET, HIGH POINTS, CHALLENGES, EXPECTATIONS VS REALITY)

THE **BEST PART** WAS...

BUDGET

$

ANTICIPATED DATE

/ / TO / /

ACTION LIST

⊘
⊘
⊘
⊘
⊘
⊘
⊘
⊘
⊘

SUCCESS!

PLACE A CHECK HERE TO
TAKE IT OFF YOUR BUCKET LIST

RATE THIS ACTIVITY

☆☆☆☆☆

THIS WOULD BE PERFECT FOR US BECAUSE...

MAKE IT HAPPEN: HOW? WHEN?

REVIEW

DATE COMPLETED: / /

WHAT HAPPENED? (PEOPLE MET, HIGH POINTS, CHALLENGES, EXPECTATIONS VS REALITY)

THE **BEST PART** WAS...

BUDGET

$

ANTICIPATED DATE

/ /   TO   / /

ACTION LIST

⊘
⊘
⊘
⊘
⊘
⊘
⊘
⊘
⊘

SUCCESS!

PLACE A CHECK HERE TO
TAKE IT OFF YOUR BUCKET LIST

RATE THIS ACTIVITY

☆☆☆☆☆

THIS WOULD BE PERFECT FOR US BECAUSE...

_____
_____
_____
_____

MAKE IT HAPPEN: HOW? WHEN?

_____
_____
_____
_____

REVIEW

DATE COMPLETED: / /

WHAT HAPPENED? (PEOPLE MET, HIGH POINTS, CHALLENGES, EXPECTATIONS VS REALITY)

_____
_____
_____
_____

THE **BEST PART** WAS...

_____
_____
_____
_____
_____

BUDGET

$

ANTICIPATED DATE

/ /   TO   / /

ACTION LIST

- ⊘
- ⊘
- ⊘
- ⊘
- ⊘
- ⊘
- ⊘
- ⊘
- ⊘

SUCCESS!

PLACE A CHECK HERE TO
TAKE IT OFF YOUR BUCKET LIST

RATE THIS ACTIVITY

☆☆☆☆☆

THIS WOULD BE PERFECT FOR US BECAUSE...

_____

_____

_____

MAKE IT HAPPEN: HOW? WHEN?

_____

_____

_____

REVIEW

DATE COMPLETED:　　/ /

WHAT HAPPENED? (PEOPLE MET, HIGH POINTS, CHALLENGES, EXPECTATIONS VS REALITY)

_____

_____

_____

THE **BEST PART** WAS...

_____

_____

_____

BUDGET

$

ANTICIPATED DATE

/ /　TO　/ /

ACTION LIST

- ⊘
- ⊘
- ⊘
- ⊘
- ⊘
- ⊘
- ⊘
- ⊘
- ⊘

SUCCESS!

PLACE A CHECK HERE TO
TAKE IT OFF YOUR BUCKET LIST

RATE THIS ACTIVITY

☆☆☆☆☆

THIS WOULD BE PERFECT FOR US BECAUSE...

_____

_____

_____

_____

MAKE IT HAPPEN: HOW? WHEN?

_____

_____

_____

_____

REVIEW

DATE COMPLETED: / /

_____

WHAT HAPPENED? (PEOPLE MET, HIGH POINTS, CHALLENGES, EXPECTATIONS VS REALITY)

_____

_____

_____

THE **BEST PART** WAS...

_____

_____

_____

_____

BUDGET

$

ANTICIPATED DATE

/ /   TO   / /

ACTION LIST

- ⊘
- ⊘
- ⊘
- ⊘
- ⊘
- ⊘
- ⊘
- ⊘
- ⊘

SUCCESS!

PLACE A CHECK HERE TO
TAKE IT OFF YOUR BUCKET LIST

RATE THIS ACTIVITY

☆☆☆☆☆

THIS WOULD BE PERFECT FOR US BECAUSE...

_____

_____

_____

_____

MAKE IT HAPPEN: HOW? WHEN?

_____

_____

_____

_____

REVIEW

DATE COMPLETED: / /

WHAT HAPPENED? (PEOPLE MET, HIGH POINTS, CHALLENGES, EXPECTATIONS VS REALITY)

_____

_____

_____

_____

THE **BEST PART** WAS...

_____

_____

_____

_____

_____

BUDGET

$

ANTICIPATED DATE

/ /   TO   / /

ACTION LIST

- ⊘
- ⊘
- ⊘
- ⊘
- ⊘
- ⊘
- ⊘
- ⊘
- ⊘

SUCCESS!

PLACE A CHECK HERE TO
TAKE IT OFF YOUR BUCKET LIST

RATE THIS ACTIVITY

☆☆☆☆☆

THIS WOULD BE PERFECT FOR US BECAUSE...

_____
_____
_____
_____

MAKE IT HAPPEN: HOW? WHEN?

_____
_____
_____
_____

REVIEW

DATE COMPLETED: /   /

WHAT HAPPENED? (PEOPLE MET, HIGH POINTS, CHALLENGES, EXPECTATIONS VS REALITY)

_____
_____
_____
_____

THE **BEST PART** WAS...

_____
_____
_____
_____
_____

BUDGET

$

ANTICIPATED DATE

/ /   TO   / /

ACTION LIST

- ⊘
- ⊘
- ⊘
- ⊘
- ⊘
- ⊘
- ⊘
- ⊘
- ⊘

SUCCESS!

PLACE A CHECK HERE TO
TAKE IT OFF YOUR BUCKET LIST

RATE THIS ACTIVITY

☆☆☆☆☆

THIS WOULD BE PERFECT FOR US BECAUSE...

_____

_____

_____

_____

MAKE IT HAPPEN: HOW? WHEN?

_____

_____

_____

_____

REVIEW

DATE COMPLETED: / /

WHAT HAPPENED? (PEOPLE MET, HIGH POINTS, CHALLENGES, EXPECTATIONS VS REALITY)

_____

_____

_____

_____

_____

THE **BEST PART** WAS...

_____

_____

_____

_____

_____

BUDGET

$

ANTICIPATED DATE

/ /   TO   / /

ACTION LIST

⊘
⊘
⊘
⊘
⊘
⊘
⊘
⊘
⊘

SUCCESS!

PLACE A CHECK HERE TO
TAKE IT OFF YOUR BUCKET LIST

RATE THIS ACTIVITY

☆☆☆☆☆

THIS WOULD BE PERFECT FOR US BECAUSE...

_____

_____

_____

_____

MAKE IT HAPPEN: HOW? WHEN?

_____

_____

_____

_____

_____

REVIEW

DATE COMPLETED: / /

WHAT HAPPENED? (PEOPLE MET, HIGH POINTS, CHALLENGES, EXPECTATIONS VS REALITY)

_____

_____

_____

_____

THE **BEST PART** WAS...

_____

_____

_____

_____

_____

BUDGET

$

ANTICIPATED DATE

/ /   TO   / /

ACTION LIST

⊘
⊘
⊘
⊘
⊘
⊘
⊘
⊘
⊘

SUCCESS!

PLACE A CHECK HERE TO
TAKE IT OFF YOUR BUCKET LIST

RATE THIS ACTIVITY

☆☆☆☆☆

THIS WOULD BE PERFECT FOR US BECAUSE...

BUDGET

$

ANTICIPATED DATE

/ /   TO   / /

MAKE IT HAPPEN: HOW? WHEN?

ACTION LIST

REVIEW

DATE COMPLETED: / /

WHAT HAPPENED? (PEOPLE MET, HIGH POINTS, CHALLENGES, EXPECTATIONS VS REALITY)

SUCCESS!

PLACE A CHECK HERE TO
TAKE IT OFF YOUR BUCKET LIST

THE **BEST PART** WAS...

RATE THIS ACTIVITY

☆☆☆☆☆

PRIORITY ☆☆☆☆☆ ITEM #29: _____

THIS WOULD BE PERFECT FOR US BECAUSE...

_____

_____

_____

_____

MAKE IT HAPPEN: HOW? WHEN?

_____

_____

_____

_____

REVIEW

DATE COMPLETED: /   /

_____

WHAT HAPPENED? (PEOPLE MET, HIGH POINTS, CHALLENGES, EXPECTATIONS VS REALITY)

_____

_____

_____

_____

_____

THE **BEST PART** WAS...

_____

_____

_____

_____

_____

BUDGET

$

ANTICIPATED DATE

/ /   TO   / /

ACTION LIST

⊘
⊘
⊘
⊘
⊘
⊘
⊘
⊘
⊘

SUCCESS!

PLACE A CHECK HERE TO
TAKE IT OFF YOUR BUCKET LIST

RATE THIS ACTIVITY

☆☆☆☆☆

THIS WOULD BE PERFECT FOR US BECAUSE...

MAKE IT HAPPEN: HOW? WHEN?

REVIEW

DATE COMPLETED: / /

WHAT HAPPENED? (PEOPLE MET, HIGH POINTS, CHALLENGES, EXPECTATIONS VS REALITY)

THE **BEST PART** WAS...

BUDGET

$

ANTICIPATED DATE

/ /   TO   / /

ACTION LIST

- ⊘
- ⊘
- ⊘
- ⊘
- ⊘
- ⊘
- ⊘
- ⊘
- ⊘

SUCCESS!

PLACE A CHECK HERE TO
TAKE IT OFF YOUR BUCKET LIST

RATE THIS ACTIVITY

☆☆☆☆☆

THIS WOULD BE PERFECT FOR US BECAUSE...	**BUDGET**

$ _____

ANTICIPATED DATE

/ /   TO   / /

MAKE IT HAPPEN: HOW? WHEN?

ACTION LIST

⊘
⊘
⊘
⊘
⊘
⊘
⊘
⊘
⊘

REVIEW

DATE COMPLETED: / /

WHAT HAPPENED? (PEOPLE MET, HIGH POINTS, CHALLENGES, EXPECTATIONS VS REALITY)

SUCCESS!

PLACE A CHECK HERE TO
TAKE IT OFF YOUR BUCKET LIST

THE **BEST PART** WAS...

RATE THIS ACTIVITY

☆☆☆☆☆

THIS WOULD BE PERFECT FOR US BECAUSE...

_____

_____

_____

_____

MAKE IT HAPPEN: HOW? WHEN?

_____

_____

_____

_____

REVIEW

DATE COMPLETED: / /

WHAT HAPPENED? (PEOPLE MET, HIGH POINTS, CHALLENGES, EXPECTATIONS VS REALITY)

_____

_____

_____

_____

THE **BEST PART** WAS...

_____

_____

_____

_____

BUDGET

$

ANTICIPATED DATE

/ /   TO   / /

ACTION LIST

- ⊘
- ⊘
- ⊘
- ⊘
- ⊘
- ⊘
- ⊘
- ⊘
- ⊘

SUCCESS!

PLACE A CHECK HERE TO
TAKE IT OFF YOUR BUCKET LIST

RATE THIS ACTIVITY

☆☆☆☆☆

PRIORITY ☆☆☆☆☆　　　ITEM #33: _____

THIS WOULD BE PERFECT FOR US BECAUSE...

_____

_____

_____

MAKE IT HAPPEN: HOW? WHEN?

_____

_____

_____

_____

REVIEW

DATE COMPLETED:　　/　/

WHAT HAPPENED? (PEOPLE MET, HIGH POINTS, CHALLENGES, EXPECTATIONS VS REALITY)

_____

_____

_____

_____

THE **BEST PART** WAS...

_____

_____

_____

_____

_____

BUDGET

$

ANTICIPATED DATE

/　/　　TO　　/　/

ACTION LIST

⊘
⊘
⊘
⊘
⊘
⊘
⊘
⊘
⊘

SUCCESS!

PLACE A CHECK HERE TO
TAKE IT OFF YOUR BUCKET LIST

RATE THIS ACTIVITY

☆☆☆☆☆

THIS WOULD BE PERFECT FOR US BECAUSE...

_____

_____

_____

MAKE IT HAPPEN: HOW? WHEN?

_____

_____

_____

_____

REVIEW

DATE COMPLETED: / /

WHAT HAPPENED? (PEOPLE MET, HIGH POINTS, CHALLENGES, EXPECTATIONS VS REALITY)

_____

_____

_____

_____

THE **BEST PART** WAS...

_____

_____

_____

_____

_____

BUDGET

$

ANTICIPATED DATE

/ /   TO   / /

ACTION LIST

⊘
⊘
⊘
⊘
⊘
⊘
⊘
⊘
⊘

SUCCESS!

PLACE A CHECK HERE TO
TAKE IT OFF YOUR BUCKET LIST

RATE THIS ACTIVITY

☆☆☆☆☆

THIS WOULD BE PERFECT FOR US BECAUSE...

_____

_____

_____

_____

MAKE IT HAPPEN: HOW? WHEN?

_____

_____

_____

_____

REVIEW

DATE COMPLETED: / /

WHAT HAPPENED? (PEOPLE MET, HIGH POINTS, CHALLENGES, EXPECTATIONS VS REALITY)

_____

_____

_____

_____

_____

THE **BEST PART** WAS...

_____

_____

_____

_____

BUDGET

$

ANTICIPATED DATE

/ /   TO   / /

ACTION LIST

⊘
⊘
⊘
⊘
⊘
⊘
⊘
⊘
⊘

SUCCESS!

PLACE A CHECK HERE TO
TAKE IT OFF YOUR BUCKET LIST

RATE THIS ACTIVITY

☆☆☆☆☆

THIS WOULD BE PERFECT FOR US BECAUSE...

_____

_____

_____

MAKE IT HAPPEN: HOW? WHEN?

_____

_____

_____

_____

REVIEW

DATE COMPLETED: / /

WHAT HAPPENED? (PEOPLE MET, HIGH POINTS, CHALLENGES, EXPECTATIONS VS REALITY)

_____

_____

_____

THE **BEST PART** WAS...

_____

_____

_____

_____

BUDGET

$

ANTICIPATED DATE

/ /   TO   / /

ACTION LIST

⊘
⊘
⊘
⊘
⊘
⊘
⊘
⊘
⊘

SUCCESS!

PLACE A CHECK HERE TO
TAKE IT OFF YOUR BUCKET LIST

RATE THIS ACTIVITY

☆☆☆☆☆

THIS WOULD BE PERFECT FOR US BECAUSE...

BUDGET

$

ANTICIPATED DATE

/ /   TO   / /

MAKE IT HAPPEN: HOW? WHEN?

ACTION LIST

⊘
⊘
⊘
⊘
⊘
⊘
⊘
⊘
⊘

REVIEW

DATE COMPLETED: / /

WHAT HAPPENED? (PEOPLE MET, HIGH POINTS, CHALLENGES, EXPECTATIONS VS REALITY)

SUCCESS!

PLACE A CHECK HERE TO
TAKE IT OFF YOUR BUCKET LIST

THE **BEST PART** WAS...

RATE THIS ACTIVITY

☆ ☆ ☆ ☆ ☆

THIS WOULD BE PERFECT FOR US BECAUSE...

_____
_____
_____
_____

MAKE IT HAPPEN: HOW? WHEN?

_____
_____
_____
_____

REVIEW

DATE COMPLETED: / /

WHAT HAPPENED? (PEOPLE MET, HIGH POINTS, CHALLENGES, EXPECTATIONS VS REALITY)

_____
_____
_____
_____

THE **BEST PART** WAS...

_____
_____
_____
_____
_____
_____

BUDGET

$

ANTICIPATED DATE

/ /   TO   / /

ACTION LIST

⊘
⊘
⊘
⊘
⊘
⊘
⊘
⊘
⊘

SUCCESS!

PLACE A CHECK HERE TO
TAKE IT OFF YOUR BUCKET LIST

RATE THIS ACTIVITY

☆☆☆☆☆

THIS WOULD BE PERFECT FOR US BECAUSE...

_____
_____
_____
_____

MAKE IT HAPPEN: HOW? WHEN?

_____
_____
_____
_____

REVIEW

DATE COMPLETED: / /

WHAT HAPPENED? (PEOPLE MET, HIGH POINTS, CHALLENGES, EXPECTATIONS VS REALITY)

_____
_____
_____
_____

THE **BEST PART** WAS...

_____
_____
_____
_____
_____

BUDGET

$

ANTICIPATED DATE

/ /   TO   / /

ACTION LIST

⊘
⊘
⊘
⊘
⊘
⊘
⊘
⊘
⊘

SUCCESS!

PLACE A CHECK HERE TO
TAKE IT OFF YOUR BUCKET LIST

RATE THIS ACTIVITY

☆☆☆☆☆

WHEN I STAND BEFORE GOD AT THE END OF MY LIFE, I WOULD HOPE THAT I WOULD NOT HAVE A SINGLE BIT OF TALENT LEFT AND COULD SAY, I USED EVERYTHING YOU GAVE ME. — ERMA BOMBECK

39

THIS WOULD BE PERFECT FOR US BECAUSE...

_____
_____
_____
_____

MAKE IT HAPPEN: HOW? WHEN?

_____
_____
_____
_____
_____

REVIEW

DATE COMPLETED: / /

WHAT HAPPENED? (PEOPLE MET, HIGH POINTS, CHALLENGES, EXPECTATIONS VS REALITY)

_____
_____
_____
_____

THE **BEST PART** WAS...

_____
_____
_____
_____
_____

BUDGET

$

ANTICIPATED DATE

/ /   TO   / /

ACTION LIST

⊘
⊘
⊘
⊘
⊘
⊘
⊘
⊘
⊘

SUCCESS!

PLACE A CHECK HERE TO
TAKE IT OFF YOUR BUCKET LIST

RATE THIS ACTIVITY

☆☆☆☆☆

THIS WOULD BE PERFECT FOR US BECAUSE...

MAKE IT HAPPEN: HOW? WHEN?

REVIEW

DATE COMPLETED: / /

WHAT HAPPENED? (PEOPLE MET, HIGH POINTS, CHALLENGES, EXPECTATIONS VS REALITY)

THE **BEST PART** WAS...

BUDGET

$

ANTICIPATED DATE

/ /   TO   / /

ACTION LIST

⊘
⊘
⊘
⊘
⊘
⊘
⊘
⊘
⊘

SUCCESS!

PLACE A CHECK HERE TO
TAKE IT OFF YOUR BUCKET LIST

RATE THIS ACTIVITY

☆☆☆☆☆

THIS WOULD BE PERFECT FOR US BECAUSE...

_____

_____

_____

MAKE IT HAPPEN: HOW? WHEN?

_____

_____

_____

_____

REVIEW

DATE COMPLETED: / /

WHAT HAPPENED? (PEOPLE MET, HIGH POINTS, CHALLENGES, EXPECTATIONS VS REALITY)

_____

_____

_____

_____

THE **BEST PART** WAS...

_____

_____

_____

_____

BUDGET

$

ANTICIPATED DATE

/ /   TO   / /

ACTION LIST

⊘
⊘
⊘
⊘
⊘
⊘
⊘
⊘
⊘

SUCCESS!

PLACE A CHECK HERE TO
TAKE IT OFF YOUR BUCKET LIST

RATE THIS ACTIVITY

☆☆☆☆☆

THIS WOULD BE PERFECT FOR US BECAUSE...

_____

_____

_____

_____

MAKE IT HAPPEN: HOW? WHEN?

_____

_____

_____

_____

REVIEW

DATE COMPLETED: / /

WHAT HAPPENED? (PEOPLE MET, HIGH POINTS, CHALLENGES, EXPECTATIONS VS REALITY)

_____

_____

_____

_____

THE **BEST PART** WAS...

_____

_____

_____

_____

_____

BUDGET

$

ANTICIPATED DATE

/ /   TO   / /

ACTION LIST

- ⊘
- ⊘
- ⊘
- ⊘
- ⊘
- ⊘
- ⊘
- ⊘
- ⊘

SUCCESS!

PLACE A CHECK HERE TO
TAKE IT OFF YOUR BUCKET LIST

RATE THIS ACTIVITY

☆☆☆☆☆

THIS WOULD BE PERFECT FOR US BECAUSE...

_____

_____

_____

_____

MAKE IT HAPPEN: HOW? WHEN?

_____

_____

_____

_____

REVIEW

DATE COMPLETED: / /

WHAT HAPPENED? (PEOPLE MET, HIGH POINTS, CHALLENGES, EXPECTATIONS VS REALITY)

_____

_____

_____

_____

THE **BEST PART** WAS...

_____

_____

_____

_____

BUDGET

$

ANTICIPATED DATE

/ /   TO   / /

ACTION LIST

- ⊘
- ⊘
- ⊘
- ⊘
- ⊘
- ⊘
- ⊘
- ⊘
- ⊘

SUCCESS!

PLACE A CHECK HERE TO
TAKE IT OFF YOUR BUCKET LIST

RATE THIS ACTIVITY

☆☆☆☆☆

THIS WOULD BE PERFECT FOR US BECAUSE...

_____

_____

_____

_____

MAKE IT HAPPEN: HOW? WHEN?

_____

_____

_____

_____

REVIEW

DATE COMPLETED: /   /

WHAT HAPPENED? (PEOPLE MET, HIGH POINTS, CHALLENGES, EXPECTATIONS VS REALITY)

_____

_____

_____

_____

THE **BEST PART** WAS...

_____

_____

_____

_____

_____

BUDGET

$

ANTICIPATED DATE

/   /   TO   /   /

ACTION LIST

⊘
⊘
⊘
⊘
⊘
⊘
⊘
⊘
⊘

SUCCESS!

PLACE A CHECK HERE TO
TAKE IT OFF YOUR BUCKET LIST

RATE THIS ACTIVITY

☆☆☆☆☆

THIS WOULD BE PERFECT FOR US BECAUSE...

_____

_____

_____

MAKE IT HAPPEN: HOW? WHEN?

_____

_____

_____

_____

REVIEW

DATE COMPLETED: / /

WHAT HAPPENED? (PEOPLE MET, HIGH POINTS, CHALLENGES, EXPECTATIONS VS REALITY)

_____

_____

_____

_____

THE **BEST PART** WAS...

_____

_____

_____

_____

BUDGET

$

ANTICIPATED DATE

/ /   TO   / /

ACTION LIST

⊘
⊘
⊘
⊘
⊘
⊘
⊘
⊘
⊘

SUCCESS!

PLACE A CHECK HERE TO
TAKE IT OFF YOUR BUCKET LIST

RATE THIS ACTIVITY

☆☆☆☆☆

THIS WOULD BE PERFECT FOR US BECAUSE...

_____

_____

_____

_____

MAKE IT HAPPEN: HOW? WHEN?

_____

_____

_____

_____

REVIEW

DATE COMPLETED: /   /

WHAT HAPPENED? (PEOPLE MET, HIGH POINTS, CHALLENGES, EXPECTATIONS VS REALITY)

_____

_____

_____

_____

_____

THE **BEST PART** WAS...

_____

_____

_____

_____

_____

BUDGET

$

ANTICIPATED DATE

/ /   TO   / /

ACTION LIST

⊘
⊘
⊘
⊘
⊘
⊘
⊘
⊘
⊘

SUCCESS!

PLACE A CHECK HERE TO
TAKE IT OFF YOUR BUCKET LIST

RATE THIS ACTIVITY

☆☆☆☆☆

ITEM #48: _____

THIS WOULD BE PERFECT FOR US BECAUSE...

_____

_____

_____

MAKE IT HAPPEN: HOW? WHEN?

_____

_____

_____

_____

REVIEW

DATE COMPLETED: / /

WHAT HAPPENED? (PEOPLE MET, HIGH POINTS, CHALLENGES, EXPECTATIONS VS REALITY)

_____

_____

_____

_____

_____

THE **BEST PART** WAS...

_____

_____

_____

_____

_____

_____

BUDGET

$

ANTICIPATED DATE

/ /   TO   / /

ACTION LIST

⊘
⊘
⊘
⊘
⊘
⊘
⊘
⊘
⊘

SUCCESS!

PLACE A CHECK HERE TO
TAKE IT OFF YOUR BUCKET LIST

RATE THIS ACTIVITY

☆☆☆☆☆

WHEN ONE DOOR OF HAPPINESS CLOSES, ANOTHER OPENS, BUT OFTEN WE LOOK SO LONG AT THE CLOSED
DOOR THAT WE DO NOT SEE THE ONE THAT HAS BEEN OPENED FOR US. — HELEN KELLER

THIS WOULD BE PERFECT FOR US BECAUSE...

BUDGET

$

MAKE IT HAPPEN: HOW? WHEN?

ANTICIPATED DATE

/ /   TO   / /

ACTION LIST

⊘
⊘
⊘
⊘
⊘
⊘
⊘
⊘
⊘

REVIEW

DATE COMPLETED: / /

WHAT HAPPENED? (PEOPLE MET, HIGH POINTS, CHALLENGES, EXPECTATIONS VS REALITY)

SUCCESS!

PLACE A CHECK HERE TO
TAKE IT OFF YOUR BUCKET LIST

THE **BEST PART** WAS...

RATE THIS ACTIVITY

☆☆☆☆☆

PRIORITY ☆☆☆☆☆   ITEM #50: _____

THIS WOULD BE PERFECT FOR US BECAUSE...

_____

_____

_____

MAKE IT HAPPEN: HOW? WHEN?

_____

_____

_____

_____

REVIEW

DATE COMPLETED: / /

WHAT HAPPENED? (PEOPLE MET, HIGH POINTS, CHALLENGES, EXPECTATIONS VS REALITY)

_____

_____

_____

_____

THE **BEST PART** WAS...

_____

_____

_____

_____

_____

BUDGET

$

ANTICIPATED DATE

/ /   TO   / /

ACTION LIST

⊘
⊘
⊘
⊘
⊘
⊘
⊘
⊘
⊘

SUCCESS!

PLACE A CHECK HERE TO
TAKE IT OFF YOUR BUCKET LIST

RATE THIS ACTIVITY

☆☆☆☆☆

THIS WOULD BE PERFECT FOR US BECAUSE...

_____

_____

_____

MAKE IT HAPPEN: HOW? WHEN?

_____

_____

_____

_____

REVIEW

DATE COMPLETED: / /

WHAT HAPPENED? (PEOPLE MET, HIGH POINTS, CHALLENGES, EXPECTATIONS VS REALITY)

_____

_____

_____

_____

THE **BEST PART** WAS...

_____

_____

_____

_____

_____

BUDGET

$

ANTICIPATED DATE

/ /   TO   / /

ACTION LIST

⊘
⊘
⊘
⊘
⊘
⊘
⊘
⊘
⊘

SUCCESS!

PLACE A CHECK HERE TO
TAKE IT OFF YOUR BUCKET LIST

RATE THIS ACTIVITY

☆☆☆☆☆

ITEM #52: _____

THIS WOULD BE PERFECT FOR US BECAUSE...

_____

_____

_____

MAKE IT HAPPEN: HOW? WHEN?

_____

_____

_____

_____

REVIEW

DATE COMPLETED: / /

WHAT HAPPENED? (PEOPLE MET, HIGH POINTS, CHALLENGES, EXPECTATIONS VS REALITY)

_____

_____

_____

_____

THE **BEST PART** WAS...

_____

_____

_____

_____

_____

BUDGET

$

ANTICIPATED DATE

/ /   TO   / /

ACTION LIST

- ⊘
- ⊘
- ⊘
- ⊘
- ⊘
- ⊘
- ⊘
- ⊘
- ⊘

SUCCESS!

PLACE A CHECK HERE TO
TAKE IT OFF YOUR BUCKET LIST

RATE THIS ACTIVITY

☆☆☆☆☆

ITEM #53: _____

THIS WOULD BE PERFECT FOR US BECAUSE...	**BUDGET**

THIS WOULD BE PERFECT FOR US BECAUSE...

_____

_____

_____

MAKE IT HAPPEN: HOW? WHEN?

_____

_____

_____

_____

REVIEW

DATE COMPLETED: /   /

WHAT HAPPENED? (PEOPLE MET, HIGH POINTS, CHALLENGES, EXPECTATIONS VS REALITY)

_____

_____

_____

_____

THE **BEST PART** WAS...

_____

_____

_____

_____

BUDGET

$

ANTICIPATED DATE

/ /   TO   / /

ACTION LIST

⊘
⊘
⊘
⊘
⊘
⊘
⊘
⊘
⊘

SUCCESS!

PLACE A CHECK HERE TO
TAKE IT OFF YOUR BUCKET LIST

RATE THIS ACTIVITY

☆☆☆☆☆

THIS WOULD BE PERFECT FOR US BECAUSE...

_____

_____

_____

MAKE IT HAPPEN: HOW? WHEN?

_____

_____

_____

REVIEW

DATE COMPLETED:　　/ /

WHAT HAPPENED? (PEOPLE MET, HIGH POINTS, CHALLENGES, EXPECTATIONS VS REALITY)

_____

_____

_____

THE **BEST PART** WAS...

_____

_____

_____

_____

BUDGET

$

ANTICIPATED DATE

/ /　　TO　　/ /

ACTION LIST

⊘
⊘
⊘
⊘
⊘
⊘
⊘
⊘
⊘

SUCCESS!

PLACE A CHECK HERE TO
TAKE IT OFF YOUR BUCKET LIST

RATE THIS ACTIVITY

☆☆☆☆☆

THIS WOULD BE PERFECT FOR US BECAUSE...

_____
_____
_____
_____

MAKE IT HAPPEN: HOW? WHEN?

_____
_____
_____
_____

REVIEW

DATE COMPLETED: / /

WHAT HAPPENED? (PEOPLE MET, HIGH POINTS, CHALLENGES, EXPECTATIONS VS REALITY)

_____
_____
_____
_____

THE **BEST PART** WAS...

_____
_____
_____
_____
_____
_____

BUDGET

$

ANTICIPATED DATE

/ /   TO   / /

ACTION LIST

○
○
○
○
○
○
○
○
○

SUCCESS!

PLACE A CHECK HERE TO
TAKE IT OFF YOUR BUCKET LIST

RATE THIS ACTIVITY

☆☆☆☆☆

FIRST, HAVE A DEFINITE, CLEAR PRACTICAL IDEAL; A GOAL, AN OBJECTIVE / SECOND, HAVE THE NECESSARY MEANS TO ACHIEVE
YOUR ENDS; WISDOM, MONEY, MATERIALS, AND METHODS / THIRD: ADJUST ALL YOUR MEANS TO THAT END. — ARISTOTLE

55

THIS WOULD BE PERFECT FOR US BECAUSE...

_____

_____

_____

_____

MAKE IT HAPPEN: HOW? WHEN?

_____

_____

_____

_____

REVIEW

DATE COMPLETED: / /

WHAT HAPPENED? (PEOPLE MET, HIGH POINTS, CHALLENGES, EXPECTATIONS VS REALITY)

_____

_____

_____

_____

THE **BEST PART** WAS...

_____

_____

_____

_____

_____

BUDGET

$

ANTICIPATED DATE

/ /   TO   / /

ACTION LIST

⊘
⊘
⊘
⊘
⊘
⊘
⊘
⊘
⊘

SUCCESS!

PLACE A CHECK HERE TO
TAKE IT OFF YOUR BUCKET LIST

RATE THIS ACTIVITY

☆☆☆☆☆

THIS WOULD BE PERFECT FOR US BECAUSE...

_____

_____

_____

_____

MAKE IT HAPPEN: HOW? WHEN?

_____

_____

_____

_____

REVIEW

DATE COMPLETED: / /

WHAT HAPPENED? (PEOPLE MET, HIGH POINTS, CHALLENGES, EXPECTATIONS VS REALITY)

_____

_____

_____

_____

THE **BEST PART** WAS...

_____

_____

_____

_____

_____

BUDGET

$

ANTICIPATED DATE

/ /   TO   / /

ACTION LIST

- ⊘
- ⊘
- ⊘
- ⊘
- ⊘
- ⊘
- ⊘
- ⊘
- ⊘

SUCCESS!

PLACE A CHECK HERE TO
TAKE IT OFF YOUR BUCKET LIST

RATE THIS ACTIVITY

☆☆☆☆☆

THIS WOULD BE PERFECT FOR US BECAUSE...

_____

_____

_____

_____

MAKE IT HAPPEN: HOW? WHEN?

_____

_____

_____

_____

REVIEW

DATE COMPLETED: / /

WHAT HAPPENED? (PEOPLE MET, HIGH POINTS, CHALLENGES, EXPECTATIONS VS REALITY)

_____

_____

_____

_____

THE **BEST PART** WAS...

_____

_____

_____

_____

BUDGET

$

ANTICIPATED DATE

/ /   TO   / /

ACTION LIST

⊘
⊘
⊘
⊘
⊘
⊘
⊘
⊘
⊘

SUCCESS!

PLACE A CHECK HERE TO
TAKE IT OFF YOUR BUCKET LIST

RATE THIS ACTIVITY

☆☆☆☆☆

WE MUST BELIEVE THAT WE ARE GIFTED FOR SOMETHING, AND THAT THIS THING, AT WHATEVER COST, MUST BE ATTAINED. — MARIE CURIE

THIS WOULD BE PERFECT FOR US BECAUSE...

_____

_____

_____

_____

MAKE IT HAPPEN: HOW? WHEN?

_____

_____

_____

_____

REVIEW

DATE COMPLETED: / /

_____

WHAT HAPPENED? (PEOPLE MET, HIGH POINTS, CHALLENGES, EXPECTATIONS VS REALITY)

_____

_____

_____

_____

THE **BEST PART** WAS...

_____

_____

_____

_____

_____

BUDGET

$

ANTICIPATED DATE

/ /   TO   / /

ACTION LIST

⊘
⊘
⊘
⊘
⊘
⊘
⊘
⊘
⊘
⊘

SUCCESS!

PLACE A CHECK HERE TO
TAKE IT OFF YOUR BUCKET LIST

RATE THIS ACTIVITY

☆☆☆☆☆

ITEM #60: _____

THIS WOULD BE PERFECT FOR US BECAUSE...

MAKE IT HAPPEN: HOW? WHEN?

REVIEW

DATE COMPLETED: / /

WHAT HAPPENED? (PEOPLE MET, HIGH POINTS, CHALLENGES, EXPECTATIONS VS REALITY)

THE **BEST PART** WAS...

BUDGET

$

ANTICIPATED DATE

/ /   TO   / /

ACTION LIST

- ⊘
- ⊘
- ⊘
- ⊘
- ⊘
- ⊘
- ⊘
- ⊘
- ⊘

SUCCESS!

PLACE A CHECK HERE TO
TAKE IT OFF YOUR BUCKET LIST

RATE THIS ACTIVITY

☆☆☆☆☆

THIS WOULD BE PERFECT FOR US BECAUSE...

_____

_____

_____

MAKE IT HAPPEN: HOW? WHEN?

_____

_____

_____

_____

REVIEW

DATE COMPLETED: / /

_____

WHAT HAPPENED? (PEOPLE MET, HIGH POINTS, CHALLENGES, EXPECTATIONS VS REALITY)

_____

_____

_____

THE **BEST PART** WAS...

_____

_____

_____

_____

_____

BUDGET

$

ANTICIPATED DATE

/ /   TO   / /

ACTION LIST

- ⊘
- ⊘
- ⊘
- ⊘
- ⊘
- ⊘
- ⊘
- ⊘
- ⊘

SUCCESS!

PLACE A CHECK HERE TO
TAKE IT OFF YOUR BUCKET LIST

RATE THIS ACTIVITY

☆☆☆☆☆

THIS WOULD BE PERFECT FOR US BECAUSE...

_____

_____

_____

_____

MAKE IT HAPPEN: HOW? WHEN?

_____

_____

_____

_____

REVIEW

DATE COMPLETED:　　/ /

WHAT HAPPENED? (PEOPLE MET, HIGH POINTS, CHALLENGES, EXPECTATIONS VS REALITY)

_____

_____

_____

_____

_____

THE **BEST PART** WAS...

_____

_____

_____

_____

_____

BUDGET

$

ANTICIPATED DATE

/ /　　TO　　/ /

ACTION LIST

⊘
⊘
⊘
⊘
⊘
⊘
⊘
⊘
⊘

SUCCESS!

PLACE A CHECK HERE TO
TAKE IT OFF YOUR BUCKET LIST

RATE THIS ACTIVITY

☆☆☆☆☆

ITEM #63: _____

THIS WOULD BE PERFECT FOR US BECAUSE...

_____

_____

_____

_____

MAKE IT HAPPEN: HOW? WHEN?

_____

_____

_____

_____

REVIEW

DATE COMPLETED: / /

WHAT HAPPENED? (PEOPLE MET, HIGH POINTS, CHALLENGES, EXPECTATIONS VS REALITY)

_____

_____

_____

_____

THE **BEST PART** WAS...

_____

_____

_____

_____

_____

BUDGET

$

ANTICIPATED DATE

/ /   TO   / /

ACTION LIST

- ⊘
- ⊘
- ⊘
- ⊘
- ⊘
- ⊘
- ⊘
- ⊘
- ⊘

SUCCESS!

PLACE A CHECK HERE TO
TAKE IT OFF YOUR BUCKET LIST

RATE THIS ACTIVITY

☆☆☆☆☆

ITEM #64: _____

THIS WOULD BE PERFECT FOR US BECAUSE...

_____

_____

_____

MAKE IT HAPPEN: HOW? WHEN?

_____

_____

_____

_____

REVIEW

DATE COMPLETED: / /

_____

WHAT HAPPENED? (PEOPLE MET, HIGH POINTS, CHALLENGES, EXPECTATIONS VS REALITY)

_____

_____

_____

_____

THE **BEST PART** WAS...

_____

_____

_____

_____

_____

BUDGET

$

ANTICIPATED DATE

/ /   TO   / /

ACTION LIST

⊘
⊘
⊘
⊘
⊘
⊘
⊘
⊘
⊘

SUCCESS!

PLACE A CHECK HERE TO
TAKE IT OFF YOUR BUCKET LIST

RATE THIS ACTIVITY

☆☆☆☆☆

ITEM #65: _____

THIS WOULD BE PERFECT FOR US BECAUSE...

_____

_____

_____

MAKE IT HAPPEN: HOW? WHEN?

_____

_____

_____

_____

REVIEW

DATE COMPLETED: / /

WHAT HAPPENED? (PEOPLE MET, HIGH POINTS, CHALLENGES, EXPECTATIONS VS REALITY)

_____

_____

_____

_____

THE **BEST PART** WAS...

_____

_____

_____

_____

_____

BUDGET

$

ANTICIPATED DATE

/ /   TO   / /

ACTION LIST

⊘
⊘
⊘
⊘
⊘
⊘
⊘
⊘
⊘

SUCCESS!

PLACE A CHECK HERE TO
TAKE IT OFF YOUR BUCKET LIST

RATE THIS ACTIVITY

☆☆☆☆☆

WHAT'S MONEY? A MAN IS A SUCCESS IF HE GETS UP IN THE MORNING AND GOES TO BED
AT NIGHT AND IN BETWEEN DOES WHAT HE WANTS TO DO. — BOB DYLAN

(65)

THIS WOULD BE PERFECT FOR US BECAUSE...

BUDGET

$

ANTICIPATED DATE

/ /   TO   / /

MAKE IT HAPPEN: HOW? WHEN?

ACTION LIST

⊘
⊘
⊘
⊘
⊘
⊘
⊘
⊘
⊘

REVIEW

DATE COMPLETED: / /

WHAT HAPPENED? (PEOPLE MET, HIGH POINTS, CHALLENGES, EXPECTATIONS VS REALITY)

SUCCESS!

PLACE A CHECK HERE TO
TAKE IT OFF YOUR BUCKET LIST

THE **BEST PART** WAS...

RATE THIS ACTIVITY

☆☆☆☆☆

PRIORITY ☆☆☆☆☆

ITEM #67: _____

	BUDGET
THIS WOULD BE PERFECT FOR US BECAUSE...	$

MAKE IT HAPPEN: HOW? WHEN?

ANTICIPATED DATE

/ / TO / /

ACTION LIST

⊘
⊘
⊘
⊘
⊘
⊘
⊘
⊘
⊘

REVIEW

DATE COMPLETED: / /

WHAT HAPPENED? (PEOPLE MET, HIGH POINTS, CHALLENGES, EXPECTATIONS VS REALITY)

SUCCESS!

PLACE A CHECK HERE TO
TAKE IT OFF YOUR BUCKET LIST

THE **BEST PART** WAS...

RATE THIS ACTIVITY

☆☆☆☆☆

THIS WOULD BE PERFECT FOR US BECAUSE...

_____

_____

_____

MAKE IT HAPPEN: HOW? WHEN?

_____

_____

_____

_____

REVIEW

DATE COMPLETED: / /

_____

WHAT HAPPENED? (PEOPLE MET, HIGH POINTS, CHALLENGES, EXPECTATIONS VS REALITY)

_____

_____

_____

_____

THE **BEST PART** WAS...

_____

_____

_____

_____

_____

BUDGET

$

ANTICIPATED DATE

/ /   TO   / /

ACTION LIST

⊘
⊘
⊘
⊘
⊘
⊘
⊘
⊘
⊘

SUCCESS!

PLACE A CHECK HERE TO
TAKE IT OFF YOUR BUCKET LIST

RATE THIS ACTIVITY

☆☆☆☆☆

THIS WOULD BE PERFECT FOR US BECAUSE...

_____

_____

_____

MAKE IT HAPPEN: HOW? WHEN?

_____

_____

_____

_____

REVIEW

DATE COMPLETED: /   /

WHAT HAPPENED? (PEOPLE MET, HIGH POINTS, CHALLENGES, EXPECTATIONS VS REALITY)

_____

_____

_____

_____

THE **BEST PART** WAS...

_____

_____

_____

_____

_____

BUDGET

$

ANTICIPATED DATE

/ /   TO   / /

ACTION LIST

⊘
⊘
⊘
⊘
⊘
⊘
⊘
⊘
⊘

SUCCESS!

PLACE A CHECK HERE TO
TAKE IT OFF YOUR BUCKET LIST

RATE THIS ACTIVITY

☆☆☆☆☆

THIS WOULD BE PERFECT FOR US BECAUSE...

_____

_____

_____

_____

MAKE IT HAPPEN: HOW? WHEN?

_____

_____

_____

_____

REVIEW

DATE COMPLETED: / /

WHAT HAPPENED? (PEOPLE MET, HIGH POINTS, CHALLENGES, EXPECTATIONS VS REALITY)

_____

_____

_____

_____

THE **BEST PART** WAS...

_____

_____

_____

_____

_____

BUDGET

$

ANTICIPATED DATE

/ /   TO   / /

ACTION LIST

- ⊘
- ⊘
- ⊘
- ⊘
- ⊘
- ⊘
- ⊘
- ⊘
- ⊘

SUCCESS!

PLACE A CHECK HERE TO
TAKE IT OFF YOUR BUCKET LIST

RATE THIS ACTIVITY

☆☆☆☆☆

PRIORITY ☆☆☆☆☆

ITEM #71: _____

THIS WOULD BE PERFECT FOR US BECAUSE...

_____

_____

_____

_____

MAKE IT HAPPEN: HOW? WHEN?

_____

_____

_____

_____

REVIEW

DATE COMPLETED: / /

WHAT HAPPENED? (PEOPLE MET, HIGH POINTS, CHALLENGES, EXPECTATIONS VS REALITY)

_____

_____

_____

_____

THE **BEST PART** WAS...

_____

_____

_____

_____

BUDGET

$

ANTICIPATED DATE

/ /   TO   / /

ACTION LIST

⊘
⊘
⊘
⊘
⊘
⊘
⊘
⊘
⊘

SUCCESS!

PLACE A CHECK HERE TO
TAKE IT OFF YOUR BUCKET LIST

RATE THIS ACTIVITY

☆☆☆☆☆

THIS WOULD BE PERFECT FOR US BECAUSE...

_____

_____

_____

MAKE IT HAPPEN: HOW? WHEN?

_____

_____

_____

REVIEW

DATE COMPLETED: / /

WHAT HAPPENED? (PEOPLE MET, HIGH POINTS, CHALLENGES, EXPECTATIONS VS REALITY)

_____

_____

_____

_____

THE **BEST PART** WAS...

_____

_____

_____

BUDGET

$

ANTICIPATED DATE

/ /   TO   / /

ACTION LIST

⊘
⊘
⊘
⊘
⊘
⊘
⊘
⊘
⊘

SUCCESS!

PLACE A CHECK HERE TO
TAKE IT OFF YOUR BUCKET LIST

RATE THIS ACTIVITY

☆☆☆☆☆

ITEM #73: _____

THIS WOULD BE PERFECT FOR US BECAUSE...

_____

_____

_____

MAKE IT HAPPEN: HOW? WHEN?

_____

_____

_____

_____

_____

REVIEW

DATE COMPLETED: / /

WHAT HAPPENED? (PEOPLE MET, HIGH POINTS, CHALLENGES, EXPECTATIONS VS REALITY)

_____

_____

_____

_____

THE **BEST PART** WAS...

_____

_____

_____

_____

_____

BUDGET

$

ANTICIPATED DATE

/ /   TO   / /

ACTION LIST

⊘
⊘
⊘
⊘
⊘
⊘
⊘
⊘
⊘

SUCCESS!

PLACE A CHECK HERE TO
TAKE IT OFF YOUR BUCKET LIST

RATE THIS ACTIVITY

☆☆☆☆☆

IT IS NOT WHAT YOU DO FOR YOUR CHILDREN, BUT WHAT YOU HAVE TAUGHT THEM TO DO FOR THEMSELVES, THAT WILL MAKE THEM SUCCESSFUL HUMAN BEINGS. — ANN LANDERS

73

ITEM #74: _____

THIS WOULD BE PERFECT FOR US BECAUSE...

_____
_____
_____
_____

MAKE IT HAPPEN: HOW? WHEN?

_____
_____
_____
_____

REVIEW

DATE COMPLETED: / /

WHAT HAPPENED? (PEOPLE MET, HIGH POINTS, CHALLENGES, EXPECTATIONS VS REALITY)

_____
_____
_____
_____

THE **BEST PART** WAS...

_____
_____
_____
_____
_____

BUDGET

$

ANTICIPATED DATE

/ /   TO   / /

ACTION LIST

- ⊘
- ⊘
- ⊘
- ⊘
- ⊘
- ⊘
- ⊘
- ⊘
- ⊘

SUCCESS!

PLACE A CHECK HERE TO
TAKE IT OFF YOUR BUCKET LIST

RATE THIS ACTIVITY

☆☆☆☆☆

IF YOU WANT YOUR CHILDREN TO TURN OUT WELL, SPEND TWICE AS MUCH TIME WITH THEM, AND HALF AS MUCH MONEY. — ABIGAIL VAN BUREN

PRIORITY ☆☆☆☆☆

ITEM #75: _____

THIS WOULD BE PERFECT FOR US BECAUSE...

_____

_____

_____

MAKE IT HAPPEN: HOW? WHEN?

_____

_____

_____

_____

REVIEW

DATE COMPLETED: / /

WHAT HAPPENED? (PEOPLE MET, HIGH POINTS, CHALLENGES, EXPECTATIONS VS REALITY)

_____

_____

_____

_____

THE **BEST PART** WAS...

_____

_____

_____

_____

BUDGET

$

ANTICIPATED DATE

/ /   TO   / /

ACTION LIST

⊘
⊘
⊘
⊘
⊘
⊘
⊘
⊘
⊘

SUCCESS!

PLACE A CHECK HERE TO
TAKE IT OFF YOUR BUCKET LIST

RATE THIS ACTIVITY

☆☆☆☆☆

THIS WOULD BE PERFECT FOR US BECAUSE...

MAKE IT HAPPEN: HOW? WHEN?

REVIEW

DATE COMPLETED: / /

WHAT HAPPENED? (PEOPLE MET, HIGH POINTS, CHALLENGES, EXPECTATIONS VS REALITY)

THE **BEST PART** WAS...

BUDGET

$

ANTICIPATED DATE

/ /   TO   / /

ACTION LIST

⊘
⊘
⊘
⊘
⊘
⊘
⊘
⊘
⊘

SUCCESS!

PLACE A CHECK HERE TO
TAKE IT OFF YOUR BUCKET LIST

RATE THIS ACTIVITY

☆☆☆☆☆

ITEM #77: _____

THIS WOULD BE PERFECT FOR US BECAUSE...	**BUDGET**
	$
	ANTICIPATED DATE
	/ / TO / /
MAKE IT HAPPEN: HOW? WHEN?	**ACTION LIST**

⊘
⊘
⊘
⊘
⊘
⊘
⊘
⊘
⊘

REVIEW

DATE COMPLETED: / /

WHAT HAPPENED? (PEOPLE MET, HIGH POINTS, CHALLENGES, EXPECTATIONS VS REALITY)

SUCCESS!

PLACE A CHECK HERE TO
TAKE IT OFF YOUR BUCKET LIST

THE **BEST PART** WAS...

RATE THIS ACTIVITY

☆☆☆☆☆

THIS WOULD BE PERFECT FOR US BECAUSE...

_____

_____

_____

MAKE IT HAPPEN: HOW? WHEN?

_____

_____

_____

_____

REVIEW

DATE COMPLETED: / /

WHAT HAPPENED? (PEOPLE MET, HIGH POINTS, CHALLENGES, EXPECTATIONS VS REALITY)

_____

_____

_____

_____

THE **BEST PART** WAS...

_____

_____

_____

_____

_____

BUDGET

$

ANTICIPATED DATE

/ /   TO   / /

ACTION LIST

⊘
⊘
⊘
⊘
⊘
⊘
⊘
⊘
⊘

SUCCESS!

PLACE A CHECK HERE TO
TAKE IT OFF YOUR BUCKET LIST

RATE THIS ACTIVITY

☆☆☆☆☆

THIS WOULD BE PERFECT FOR US BECAUSE...

_____
_____
_____
_____

MAKE IT HAPPEN: HOW? WHEN?

_____
_____
_____
_____

REVIEW

DATE COMPLETED: / /

WHAT HAPPENED? (PEOPLE MET, HIGH POINTS, CHALLENGES, EXPECTATIONS VS REALITY)

_____
_____
_____
_____

THE **BEST PART** WAS...

_____
_____
_____
_____
_____

BUDGET

$

ANTICIPATED DATE

/ /   TO   / /

ACTION LIST

⊘
⊘
⊘
⊘
⊘
⊘
⊘
⊘
⊘

SUCCESS!

PLACE A CHECK HERE TO
TAKE IT OFF YOUR BUCKET LIST

RATE THIS ACTIVITY

☆☆☆☆☆

PRIORITY ☆☆☆☆☆   ITEM #80: _____

THIS WOULD BE PERFECT FOR US BECAUSE...

_____

_____

_____

_____

MAKE IT HAPPEN: HOW? WHEN?

_____

_____

_____

_____

REVIEW

DATE COMPLETED: / /

WHAT HAPPENED? (PEOPLE MET, HIGH POINTS, CHALLENGES, EXPECTATIONS VS REALITY)

_____

_____

_____

_____

THE **BEST PART** WAS...

_____

_____

_____

_____

_____

BUDGET

$

ANTICIPATED DATE

/ /   TO   / /

ACTION LIST

- ⊘
- ⊘
- ⊘
- ⊘
- ⊘
- ⊘
- ⊘
- ⊘
- ⊘

SUCCESS!

PLACE A CHECK HERE TO
TAKE IT OFF YOUR BUCKET LIST

RATE THIS ACTIVITY

☆☆☆☆☆

THIS WOULD BE PERFECT FOR US BECAUSE...

_____

_____

_____

_____

MAKE IT HAPPEN: HOW? WHEN?

_____

_____

_____

_____

REVIEW

DATE COMPLETED:　　/　/

_____

WHAT HAPPENED? (PEOPLE MET, HIGH POINTS, CHALLENGES, EXPECTATIONS VS REALITY)

_____

_____

_____

_____

THE **BEST PART** WAS...

_____

_____

_____

_____

_____

BUDGET

$

ANTICIPATED DATE

/　/　　TO　　/　/

ACTION LIST

- ⊘
- ⊘
- ⊘
- ⊘
- ⊘
- ⊘
- ⊘
- ⊘
- ⊘

SUCCESS!

PLACE A CHECK HERE TO
TAKE IT OFF YOUR BUCKET LIST

RATE THIS ACTIVITY

☆☆☆☆☆

THIS WOULD BE PERFECT FOR US BECAUSE...

MAKE IT HAPPEN: HOW? WHEN?

REVIEW

DATE COMPLETED: / /

WHAT HAPPENED? (PEOPLE MET, HIGH POINTS, CHALLENGES, EXPECTATIONS VS REALITY)

THE **BEST PART** WAS...

BUDGET

$

ANTICIPATED DATE

/ /   TO   / /

ACTION LIST

⊘
⊘
⊘
⊘
⊘
⊘
⊘
⊘
⊘

SUCCESS!

PLACE A CHECK HERE TO
TAKE IT OFF YOUR BUCKET LIST

RATE THIS ACTIVITY

☆☆☆☆☆

PRIORITY ☆☆☆☆☆

ITEM #83: _____

	BUDGET
THIS WOULD BE PERFECT FOR US BECAUSE...	$

ANTICIPATED DATE

/ /   TO   / /

MAKE IT HAPPEN: HOW? WHEN?

ACTION LIST

⊘
⊘
⊘
⊘
⊘
⊘
⊘
⊘
⊘

REVIEW

DATE COMPLETED: / /

WHAT HAPPENED? (PEOPLE MET, HIGH POINTS, CHALLENGES, EXPECTATIONS VS REALITY)

SUCCESS!

PLACE A CHECK HERE TO
TAKE IT OFF YOUR BUCKET LIST

THE **BEST PART** WAS...

RATE THIS ACTIVITY

☆☆☆☆☆

PRIORITY ☆☆☆☆☆   ITEM #84: _____

THIS WOULD BE PERFECT FOR US BECAUSE...	**BUDGET**
	$
	ANTICIPATED DATE
	/ / TO / /
MAKE IT HAPPEN: HOW? WHEN?	**ACTION LIST**

THIS WOULD BE PERFECT FOR US BECAUSE...
_____
_____
_____

MAKE IT HAPPEN: HOW? WHEN?
_____
_____
_____
_____

REVIEW

DATE COMPLETED: / /

WHAT HAPPENED? (PEOPLE MET, HIGH POINTS, CHALLENGES, EXPECTATIONS VS REALITY)
_____
_____
_____
_____

THE **BEST PART** WAS...
_____
_____
_____
_____
_____

BUDGET

$

ANTICIPATED DATE

/ /   TO   / /

ACTION LIST

⊘
⊘
⊘
⊘
⊘
⊘
⊘
⊘
⊘

SUCCESS!

PLACE A CHECK HERE TO
TAKE IT OFF YOUR BUCKET LIST

RATE THIS ACTIVITY

☆☆☆☆☆

(84)

OUR LIVES BEGIN TO END THE DAY WE BECOME SILENT ABOUT THINGS THAT MATTER. — MARTIN LUTHER KING JR.

PRIORITY ☆☆☆☆☆　　　　　ITEM #85: _____

THIS WOULD BE PERFECT FOR US BECAUSE...	**BUDGET**
	$
	ANTICIPATED DATE
MAKE IT HAPPEN: HOW? WHEN?	/ /　TO　/ /
	ACTION LIST
	⊘
	⊘
	⊘
	⊘
# REVIEW	⊘
	⊘
DATE COMPLETED:　　/ /	⊘
	⊘
	⊘
WHAT HAPPENED? (PEOPLE MET, HIGH POINTS, CHALLENGES, EXPECTATIONS VS REALITY)	
	SUCCESS!
	PLACE A CHECK HERE TO TAKE IT OFF YOUR BUCKET LIST
THE **BEST PART** WAS...	**RATE THIS ACTIVITY**
	☆☆☆☆☆

THIS WOULD BE PERFECT FOR US BECAUSE...

_____

_____

_____

MAKE IT HAPPEN: HOW? WHEN?

_____

_____

_____

_____

REVIEW

DATE COMPLETED: / /

WHAT HAPPENED? (PEOPLE MET, HIGH POINTS, CHALLENGES, EXPECTATIONS VS REALITY)

_____

_____

_____

_____

THE **BEST PART** WAS...

_____

_____

_____

_____

_____

_____

BUDGET

$

ANTICIPATED DATE

/ /   TO   / /

ACTION LIST

⊘

⊘

⊘

⊘

⊘

⊘

⊘

⊘

⊘

SUCCESS!

PLACE A CHECK HERE TO
TAKE IT OFF YOUR BUCKET LIST

RATE THIS ACTIVITY

☆☆☆☆☆

ITEM #87: _____

THIS WOULD BE PERFECT FOR US BECAUSE...

_____
_____
_____
_____

MAKE IT HAPPEN: HOW? WHEN?

_____
_____
_____
_____

REVIEW

DATE COMPLETED: / /

WHAT HAPPENED? (PEOPLE MET, HIGH POINTS, CHALLENGES, EXPECTATIONS VS REALITY)

_____
_____
_____
_____

THE **BEST PART** WAS...

_____
_____
_____
_____
_____

BUDGET

$

ANTICIPATED DATE

/ /   TO   / /

ACTION LIST

⊘
⊘
⊘
⊘
⊘
⊘
⊘
⊘
⊘

SUCCESS!

PLACE A CHECK HERE TO
TAKE IT OFF YOUR BUCKET LIST

RATE THIS ACTIVITY

☆☆☆☆☆

PRIORITY ☆☆☆☆☆

ITEM #88: _____

THIS WOULD BE PERFECT FOR US BECAUSE...

_____
_____
_____
_____

MAKE IT HAPPEN: HOW? WHEN?

_____
_____
_____
_____

REVIEW

DATE COMPLETED: ___ / ___ / ___

WHAT HAPPENED? (PEOPLE MET, HIGH POINTS, CHALLENGES, EXPECTATIONS VS REALITY)

_____
_____
_____
_____

THE **BEST PART** WAS...

_____
_____
_____
_____
_____

BUDGET

$

ANTICIPATED DATE

___ / ___ TO ___ / ___

ACTION LIST

⊘
⊘
⊘
⊘
⊘
⊘
⊘
⊘
⊘

SUCCESS!

PLACE A CHECK HERE TO
TAKE IT OFF YOUR BUCKET LIST

RATE THIS ACTIVITY

☆☆☆☆☆

IT'S YOUR PLACE IN THE WORLD; IT'S YOUR LIFE... GO ON AND DO ALL YOU CAN WITH IT, AND MAKE IT THE LIFE YOU WANT TO LIVE. — MAE JEMISON

ITEM #89: _____

THIS WOULD BE PERFECT FOR US BECAUSE...

_____

_____

_____

MAKE IT HAPPEN: HOW? WHEN?

_____

_____

_____

_____

REVIEW

DATE COMPLETED: / /

WHAT HAPPENED? (PEOPLE MET, HIGH POINTS, CHALLENGES, EXPECTATIONS VS REALITY)

_____

_____

_____

_____

THE **BEST PART** WAS...

_____

_____

_____

_____

_____

BUDGET

$ _____

ANTICIPATED DATE

/ /   TO   / /

ACTION LIST

⊘ _____
⊘ _____
⊘ _____
⊘ _____
⊘ _____
⊘ _____
⊘ _____
⊘ _____
⊘ _____

SUCCESS!

PLACE A CHECK HERE TO
TAKE IT OFF YOUR BUCKET LIST

RATE THIS ACTIVITY

☆☆☆☆☆

THIS WOULD BE PERFECT FOR US BECAUSE...

_____

_____

_____

MAKE IT HAPPEN: HOW? WHEN?

_____

_____

_____

_____

REVIEW

DATE COMPLETED: / /

WHAT HAPPENED? (PEOPLE MET, HIGH POINTS, CHALLENGES, EXPECTATIONS VS REALITY)

_____

_____

_____

_____

THE **BEST PART** WAS...

_____

_____

_____

_____

_____

BUDGET

$

ANTICIPATED DATE

/ /   TO   / /

ACTION LIST

⊘
⊘
⊘
⊘
⊘
⊘
⊘
⊘
⊘

SUCCESS!

PLACE A CHECK HERE TO
TAKE IT OFF YOUR BUCKET LIST

RATE THIS ACTIVITY

☆☆☆☆☆

ITEM #91: _____

THIS WOULD BE PERFECT FOR US BECAUSE...	**BUDGET**
	$
	ANTICIPATED DATE
	/ / TO / /

MAKE IT HAPPEN: HOW? WHEN?

ACTION LIST

⊘
⊘
⊘
⊘
⊘
⊘
⊘
⊘
⊘

REVIEW

DATE COMPLETED: / /

WHAT HAPPENED? (PEOPLE MET, HIGH POINTS, CHALLENGES, EXPECTATIONS VS REALITY)

SUCCESS!

PLACE A CHECK HERE TO
TAKE IT OFF YOUR BUCKET LIST

THE **BEST PART** WAS...

RATE THIS ACTIVITY

☆☆☆☆☆

THIS WOULD BE PERFECT FOR US BECAUSE...

_____

_____

_____

_____

MAKE IT HAPPEN: HOW? WHEN?

_____

_____

_____

_____

REVIEW

DATE COMPLETED: /   /

WHAT HAPPENED? (PEOPLE MET, HIGH POINTS, CHALLENGES, EXPECTATIONS VS REALITY)

_____

_____

_____

_____

THE **BEST PART** WAS...

_____

_____

_____

_____

_____

BUDGET

$

ANTICIPATED DATE

/ /   TO   / /

ACTION LIST

⊘
⊘
⊘
⊘
⊘
⊘
⊘
⊘
⊘

SUCCESS!

PLACE A CHECK HERE TO
TAKE IT OFF YOUR BUCKET LIST

RATE THIS ACTIVITY

☆ ☆ ☆ ☆ ☆

ITEM #93: _____

THIS WOULD BE PERFECT FOR US BECAUSE...

_____
_____
_____
_____

MAKE IT HAPPEN: HOW? WHEN?

_____
_____
_____
_____
_____

REVIEW

DATE COMPLETED: / /

_____

WHAT HAPPENED? (PEOPLE MET, HIGH POINTS, CHALLENGES, EXPECTATIONS VS REALITY)

_____
_____
_____
_____
_____

THE **BEST PART** WAS...

_____
_____
_____
_____
_____

BUDGET

$

ANTICIPATED DATE

/ / TO / /

ACTION LIST

⊘
⊘
⊘
⊘
⊘
⊘
⊘
⊘
⊘

SUCCESS!

PLACE A CHECK HERE TO
TAKE IT OFF YOUR BUCKET LIST

RATE THIS ACTIVITY

☆☆☆☆☆

PRIORITY ☆☆☆☆☆   ITEM #94: _____

THIS WOULD BE PERFECT FOR US BECAUSE...	**BUDGET**
	$

ANTICIPATED DATE

/ /   TO   / /

MAKE IT HAPPEN: HOW? WHEN?

ACTION LIST

⊘
⊘
⊘
⊘
⊘
⊘
⊘
⊘
⊘

REVIEW

DATE COMPLETED: / /

WHAT HAPPENED? (PEOPLE MET, HIGH POINTS, CHALLENGES, EXPECTATIONS VS REALITY)

SUCCESS!

PLACE A CHECK HERE TO
TAKE IT OFF YOUR BUCKET LIST

THE **BEST PART** WAS...

RATE THIS ACTIVITY

☆☆☆☆☆

ITEM #95: _____

THIS WOULD BE PERFECT FOR US BECAUSE...	**BUDGET**
	$

MAKE IT HAPPEN: HOW? WHEN?

ANTICIPATED DATE

/ /   TO   / /

ACTION LIST

- ⊘
- ⊘
- ⊘
- ⊘
- ⊘
- ⊘
- ⊘
- ⊘
- ⊘

REVIEW

DATE COMPLETED: / /

WHAT HAPPENED? (PEOPLE MET, HIGH POINTS, CHALLENGES, EXPECTATIONS VS REALITY)

SUCCESS!

PLACE A CHECK HERE TO
TAKE IT OFF YOUR BUCKET LIST

THE **BEST PART** WAS...

RATE THIS ACTIVITY

☆☆☆☆☆

THIS WOULD BE PERFECT FOR US BECAUSE...

BUDGET
$

ANTICIPATED DATE
/ / TO / /

MAKE IT HAPPEN: HOW? WHEN?

ACTION LIST

⊘
⊘
⊘
⊘
⊘
⊘
⊘
⊘
⊘

REVIEW

DATE COMPLETED: / /

WHAT HAPPENED? (PEOPLE MET, HIGH POINTS, CHALLENGES, EXPECTATIONS VS REALITY)

SUCCESS!

PLACE A CHECK HERE TO
TAKE IT OFF YOUR BUCKET LIST

THE **BEST PART** WAS...

RATE THIS ACTIVITY

☆☆☆☆☆

PRIORITY ☆☆☆☆☆

ITEM #97: _____

	BUDGET
THIS WOULD BE PERFECT FOR US BECAUSE...	$

THIS WOULD BE PERFECT FOR US BECAUSE...

_____
_____
_____
_____

ANTICIPATED DATE

/ /   TO   / /

MAKE IT HAPPEN: HOW? WHEN?

_____
_____
_____
_____
_____

ACTION LIST

⊘
⊘
⊘
⊘
⊘
⊘
⊘
⊘
⊘

REVIEW

DATE COMPLETED: / /

_____

WHAT HAPPENED? (PEOPLE MET, HIGH POINTS, CHALLENGES, EXPECTATIONS VS REALITY)

_____
_____
_____
_____

(**SUCCESS!**)

PLACE A CHECK HERE TO
TAKE IT OFF YOUR BUCKET LIST

THE **BEST PART** WAS...

_____
_____
_____
_____
_____

RATE THIS ACTIVITY

☆☆☆☆☆

SOMEONE IS SITTING IN THE SHADE TODAY BECAUSE SOMEONE PLANTED A TREE A LONG TIME AGO. —WARREN BUFFETT

THIS WOULD BE PERFECT FOR US BECAUSE...

_____

_____

_____

MAKE IT HAPPEN: HOW? WHEN?

_____

_____

_____

_____

REVIEW

DATE COMPLETED: / /

WHAT HAPPENED? (PEOPLE MET, HIGH POINTS, CHALLENGES, EXPECTATIONS VS REALITY)

_____

_____

_____

_____

THE **BEST PART** WAS...

_____

_____

_____

_____

_____

BUDGET

$

ANTICIPATED DATE

/ /   TO   / /

ACTION LIST

⊘
⊘
⊘
⊘
⊘
⊘
⊘
⊘
⊘

SUCCESS!

PLACE A CHECK HERE TO
TAKE IT OFF YOUR BUCKET LIST

RATE THIS ACTIVITY

☆☆☆☆☆

THIS WOULD BE PERFECT FOR US BECAUSE...

_____

_____

_____

_____

MAKE IT HAPPEN: HOW? WHEN?

_____

_____

_____

_____

_____

REVIEW

DATE COMPLETED: / /

_____

WHAT HAPPENED? (PEOPLE MET, HIGH POINTS, CHALLENGES, EXPECTATIONS VS REALITY)

_____

_____

_____

_____

_____

THE **BEST PART** WAS...

_____

_____

_____

_____

_____

_____

BUDGET

$

ANTICIPATED DATE

/ /   TO   / /

ACTION LIST

⊘
⊘
⊘
⊘
⊘
⊘
⊘
⊘
⊘

SUCCESS!

PLACE A CHECK HERE TO
TAKE IT OFF YOUR BUCKET LIST

RATE THIS ACTIVITY

☆☆☆☆☆

THIS WOULD BE PERFECT FOR US BECAUSE...

MAKE IT HAPPEN: HOW? WHEN?

REVIEW

DATE COMPLETED: / /

WHAT HAPPENED? (PEOPLE MET, HIGH POINTS, CHALLENGES, EXPECTATIONS VS REALITY)

THE **BEST PART** WAS...

BUDGET

$

ANTICIPATED DATE

/ /   TO   / /

ACTION LIST

⊘
⊘
⊘
⊘
⊘
⊘
⊘
⊘
⊘

SUCCESS!

PLACE A CHECK HERE TO
TAKE IT OFF YOUR BUCKET LIST

RATE THIS ACTIVITY

☆☆☆☆☆

PRIORITY ☆☆☆☆☆   ITEM #101: _____

THIS WOULD BE PERFECT FOR US BECAUSE...	**BUDGET**
	$

MAKE IT HAPPEN: HOW? WHEN?

ANTICIPATED DATE

/ /   TO   / /

ACTION LIST

⊘
⊘
⊘
⊘
⊘
⊘
⊘
⊘
⊘

REVIEW

DATE COMPLETED: / /

WHAT HAPPENED? (PEOPLE MET, HIGH POINTS, CHALLENGES, EXPECTATIONS VS REALITY)

THE **BEST PART** WAS...

SUCCESS!

PLACE A CHECK HERE TO
TAKE IT OFF YOUR BUCKET LIST

RATE THIS ACTIVITY

☆☆☆☆☆

Ordering Information
Order more copies of this title at
bit.ly/SuperiorNotebooks

Publisher's Cataloging-in-Publication data
Superior Notebooks.
Our Bucket List: An Anniversary Gift For Both Of Us.
Bucket List For Couples · Romantic Activity Planner
Journal / Superior Notebooks.
p. cm.

ISBN 9781090409928

1. Marriage. 2. Psychological recreations. 3. Self-
actualization (Psychology).--Examinations, questions,
etc. I. Superior Notebooks. II. Title.

Printed in Poland
by Amazon Fulfillment
Poland Sp. z o.o., Wrocław

58488898R00063